I0813941

17
5
p
5
3
2
4

21

25
1
f
2

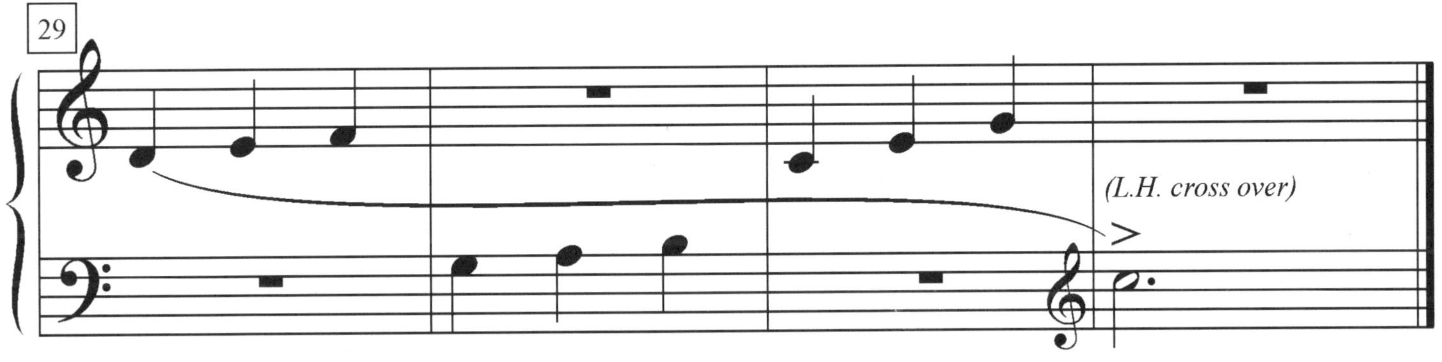
29
(L.H. cross over)

Bubble Gum

Music by Alice M. McCullen
Words by John W. Schaum

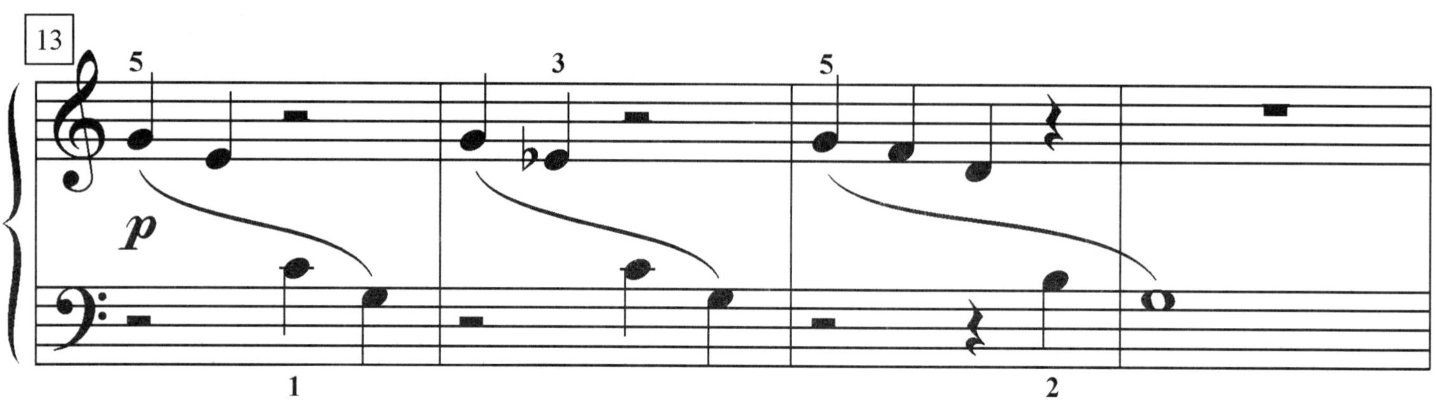

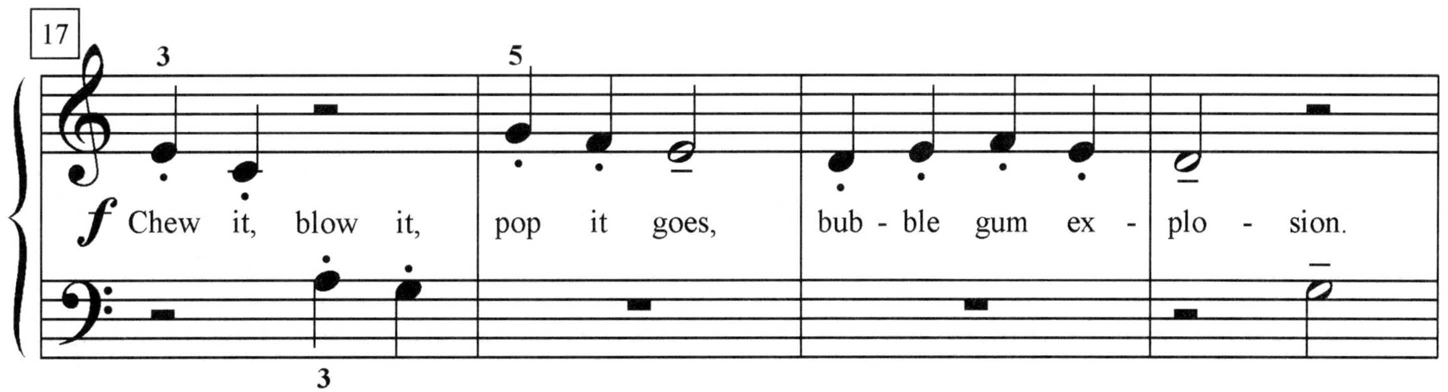
17
3
5
f
Chew it, blow it, pop it goes, bub - ble gum ex - plo - sion.
3

21
'Care - ful it might hit your nose. Keep it off your clothes! (Pop)
2
(L.H. cross over)

25
1
Buy some bub - ble gum. Then we'll have a lot of fun.
1

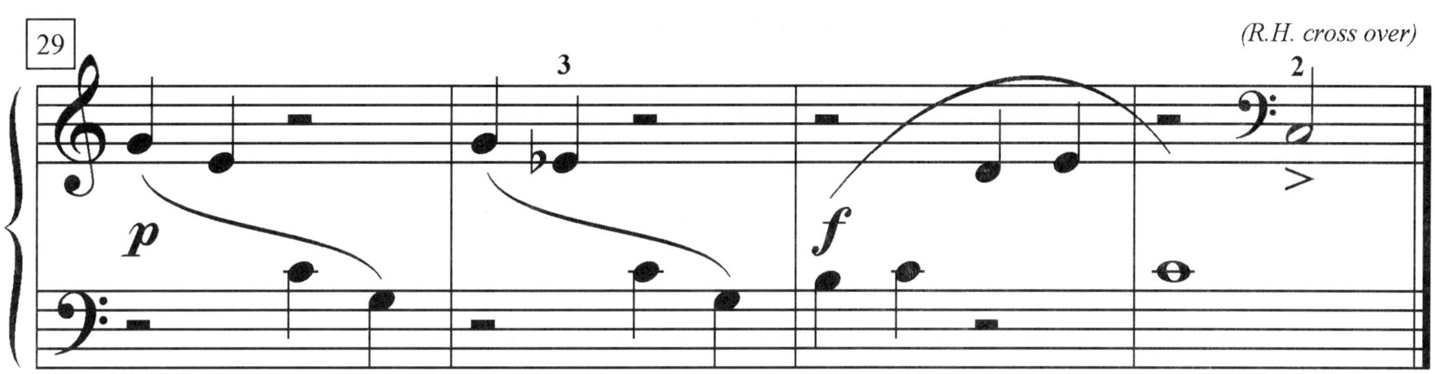
29
(R.H. cross over)
3
2
p
f

Scrambled Eggs*

Wesley Schaum and
Margarite E. Schmidt

* How many places can you find the word ***EGG*** spelled out in the music notes? Also look for the word ***EGG*** spelled backwards (GGE). Two of the measures are marked for you.

Tick Tack Toe

* D.C. al Fine is the abbreviation for ***da capo al fine*** (dah-KAH-poh ahl FEE-nay). It means go back to the beginning, repeat and stop at the word ***fine***, which means the end.

Penguins at Play

Music by Julia Heim
Words by John W. Schaum

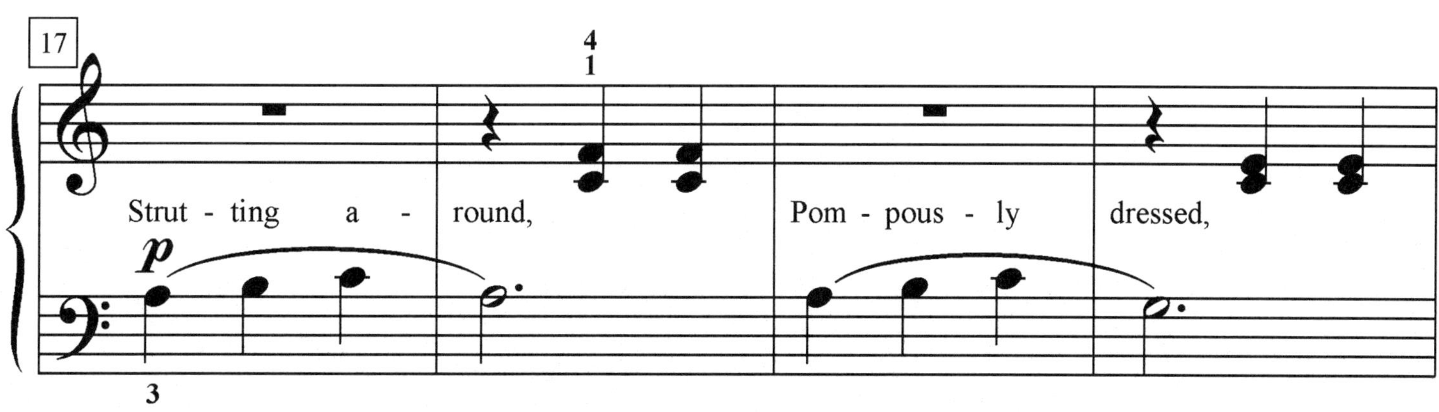
17
4
1
Strut - ting a - round,
Pom - pous - ly dressed,
p
3

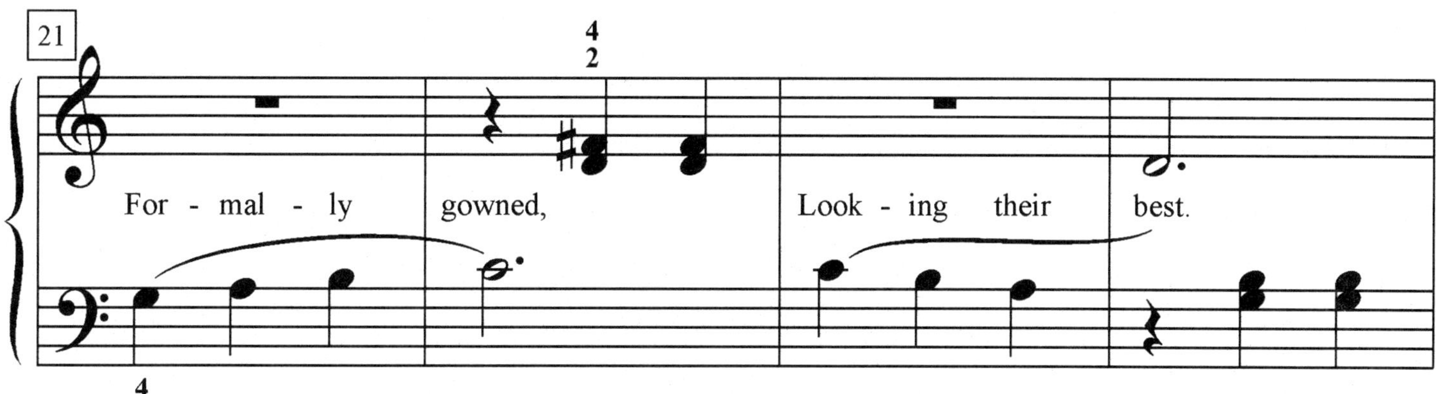
21
4
2
For - mal - ly gowned,
Look - ing their best.
4

25
Pen - guins are slick.
They're full of tricks.
f

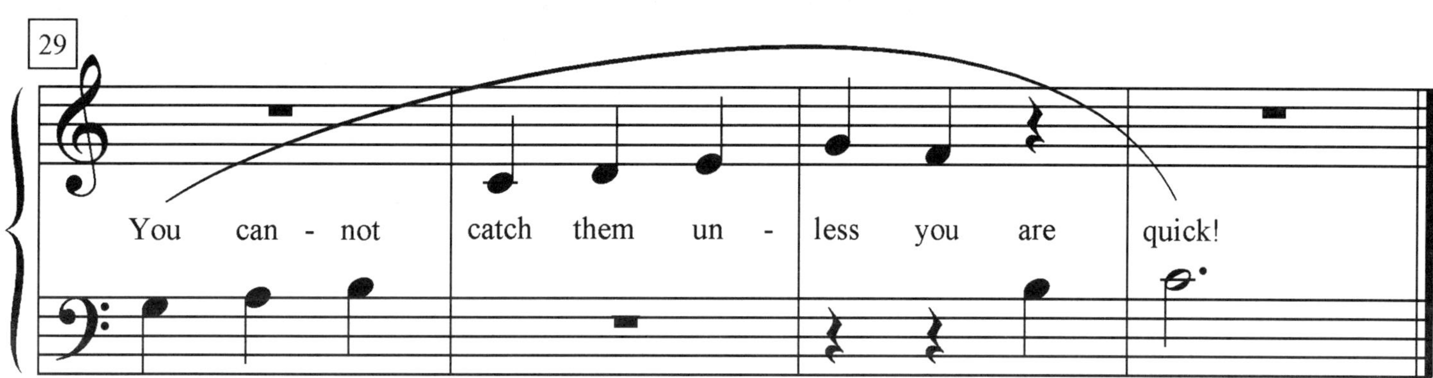
29
You can - not catch them un - less you are quick!

Bike Hike

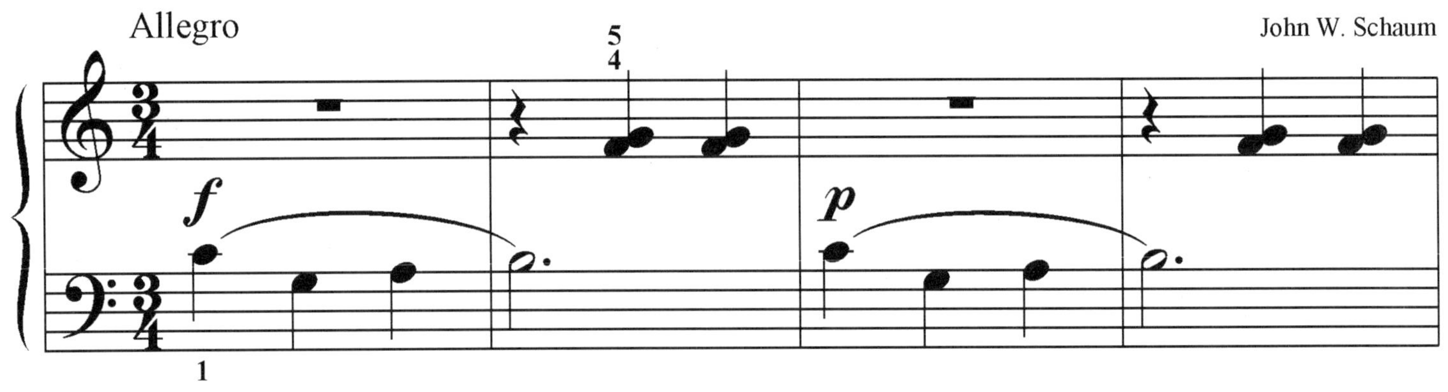

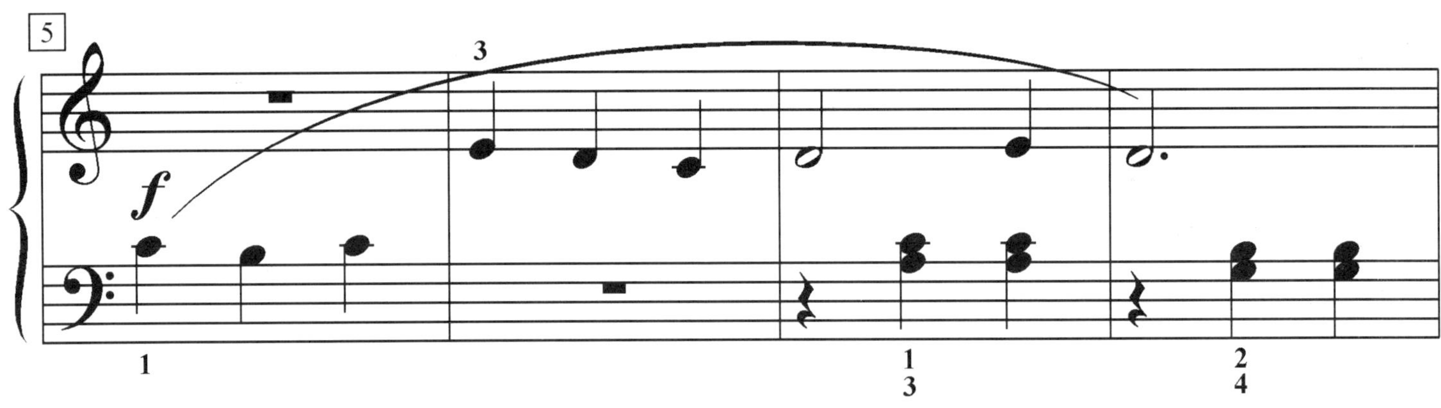

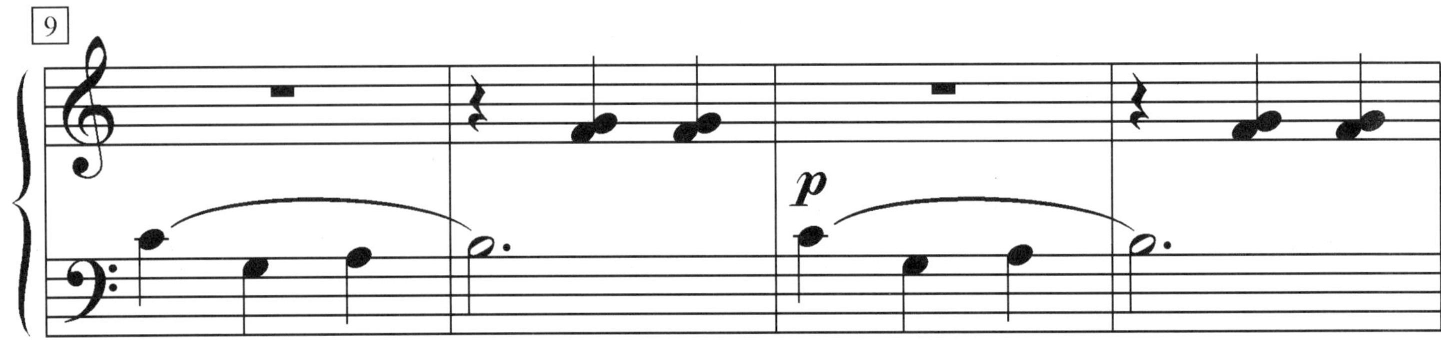

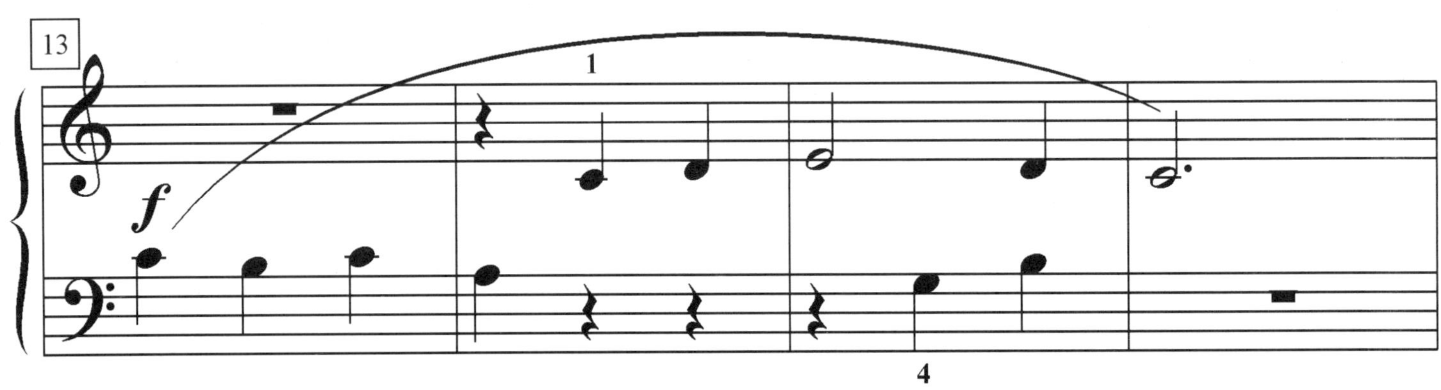

17
2
4
2
2
4
21
p
1
3
25
5
4
f
1
p
29
1
f

EXCLUSIVELY
DISTRIBUTED BY
HAL LEONARD
00645109 0 08148 01700 3
U.S. $4.95
1700

ISBN-13: 978-1-4950-8079-1
Distributed By
HAL LEONARD
00645109 9 781495 080791

$4.95
17-00

Lollipop Waltz

Andante

John W. Schaum

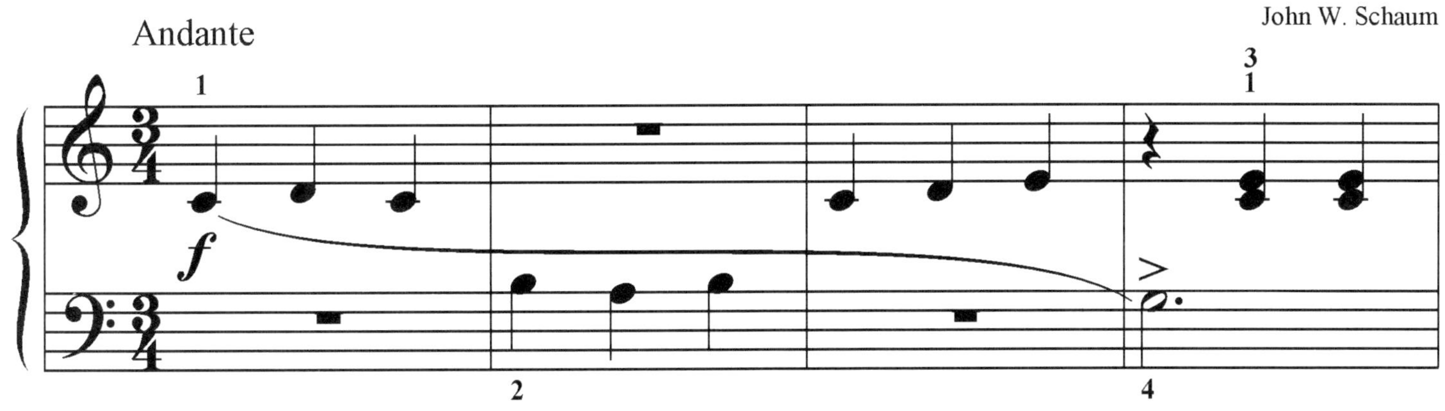

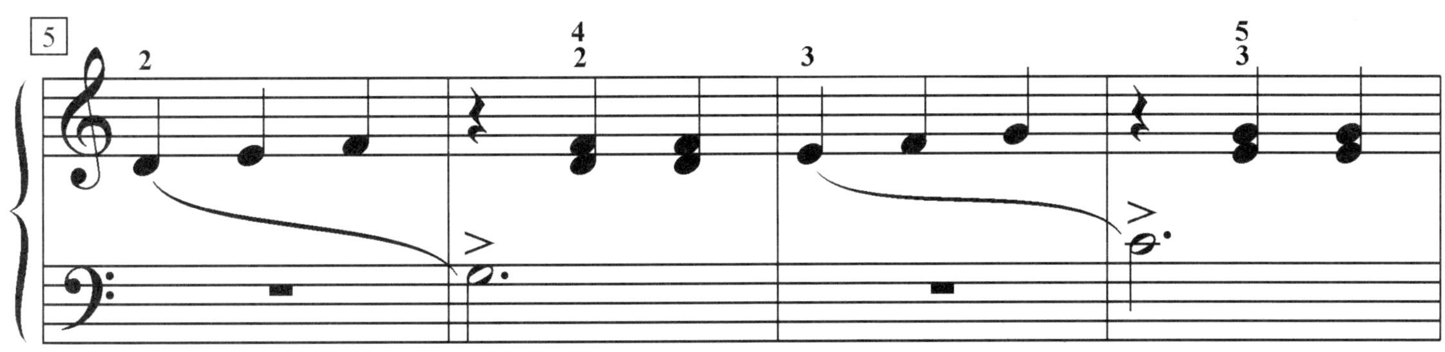

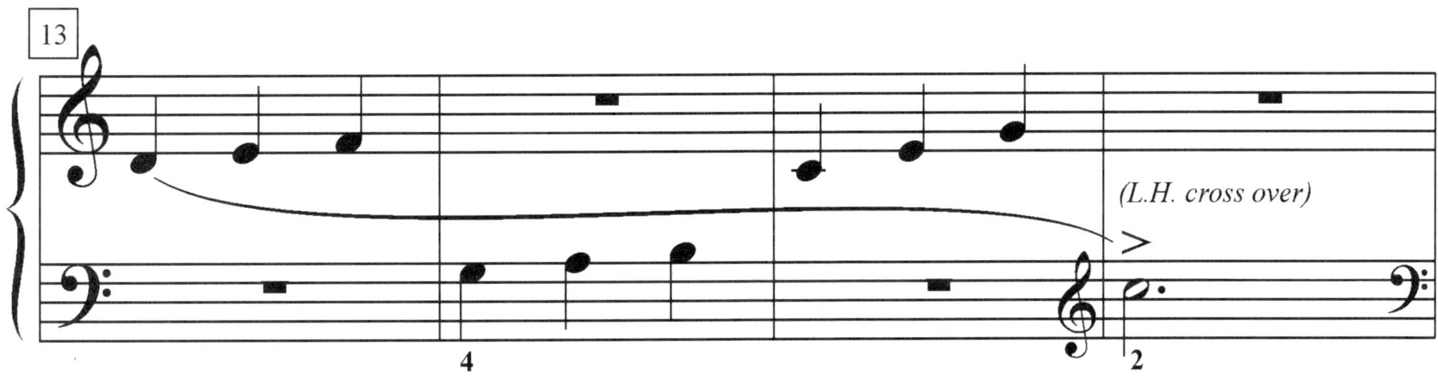

Schaum

Festival of Solos

6 Favorites in a Variety of Styles

Primer Level

Early Elementary

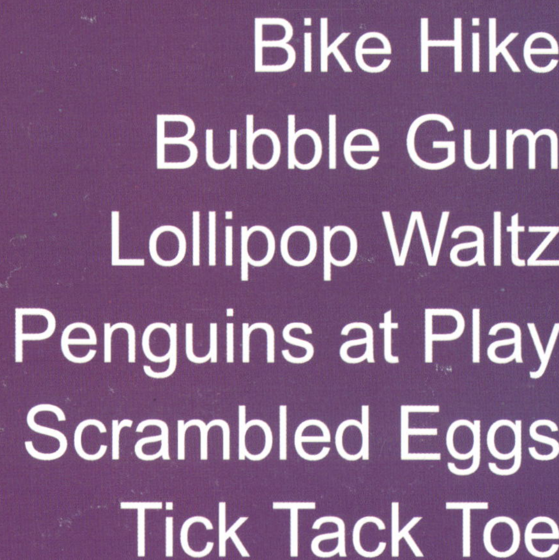

Bike Hike

Bubble Gum

Lollipop Waltz

Penguins at Play

Scrambled Eggs

Tick Tack Toe

Schaum - Festival of Solos, Primer Level

17-00